Reducing Air Pollution

Jen Green

GARETH**STEVENS**
PUBLISHING
A World Almanac Education Group Company

Please visit our web site at: www.garethstevens.com
For a free color catalog describing Gareth Stevens Publishing's list of high-quality books
and multimedia programs, call 1-800-542-2595 (USA) or 1-800-387-3178 (Canada).
Gareth Stevens Publishing's fax: (414) 332-3567.

Library of Congress Cataloging-in-Publication Data

Green, Jen.
    Reducing air pollution / Jen Green.
        p. cm. — (Improving our environment)
    Includes bibliographical references and index.
    ISBN 0-8368-4428-9 (lib. bdg.)
    Contents: Vital air — Natural cycles — What causes pollution? — Industry and energy —
Traffic pollution — Smoggy cities — Acid rain — Global warming — Changing weather —
Ozone loss — The global threat — Tackling air pollution — Get involved!
    1. Air—Pollution—Juvenile literature.   2. Air quality management—Juvenile literature.
I. Title. II. Series.
    TD883.13.G76   2005
    363.739'2—dc22   2004056595

This North American edition first published in 2005 by
Gareth Stevens Publishing
A World Almanac Education Group Company
330 West Olive Street, Suite 100
Milwaukee, WI 53212 USA

This U.S. edition copyright © 2005 by Gareth Stevens, Inc. Original edition copyright © 2005 by
Hodder Wayland. First published in 2005 by Hodder Wayland, an imprint of Hodder Children's Books,
a division of Hodder Headline Limited, 338 Euston Road, London NW1 3BH, U.K.

Series Editor: Victoria Brooker
Editor: Patience Coster
Designer: Fiona Webb
Artwork: Peter Bull
Gareth Stevens Editor: Carol Ryback
Gareth Stevens Designer: Steve Schraenkler

Photo credits: (t)top, (b) bottom, (l)left, (r) right
CORBIS: Reuters/Colin Braley 12. Ecoscene: Alex Bartel title page, 9; Angela Hampton 4, 10; Anthony
Harrison 7; Andrew Brown 14; Graham Kitching 19. Edward Parker 15. Frank Lane Picture Agency:
Jurgen and Christine Sohns 6; Terry Whittaker 13; Rolf Bender 16; Michael Gore 25. Science Photo Library:
NASA/Science Photo Library 22. Still Pictures: Ron Giling 5; Nigel Dickinson 8, 20; Mark Edwards 17;
Klause Andrews 18; Sergio Hanquet 21; Anuke Maslennikov 23; David Woodfall 26–27(b); Martin Bond 27(t).
Topham Picturepoint: Colin Pickerell/The Image Works 11, 24, 28; Bob Daemmrich/The Image Works 29.

Printed in China

1 2 3 4 5 6 7 8 9 09 08 07 06 05

Contents

Words in **bold** can be found in the glossary.

Vital Air

The air in Earth's atmosphere is vital to living things. Nature can produce some **pollution**, but people and their machines also cause much of the pollution that harms the air and damages the natural world.

A layer of gases, called Earth's atmosphere, surrounds our planet like a blanket. The main gas in the atmosphere is nitrogen. Oxygen, which animals need to breathe, makes up only one-fifth of Earth's atmosphere. The concentration of the different atmospheric gases is uneven and stronger near Earth's surface than the gas concentrations higher up.

Animals, including people, need a continuous supply of clean air. ▼

▲ Most air pollution comes from vehicles (such as buses, cars, and airplanes), **power plants**, and factories — like this one in Brazil.

Polluted Air

People pollute (dirty) the clean, fresh air in Earth's atmosphere. As we burn fuel in our vehicles, homes, and factories, we add poisonous gases to the atmosphere. Air pollution harms life on Earth. Many scientists believe that air pollution is changing our weather patterns and climate.

TRY THIS!

The Lichen (pronounced "like-in") Test

How clean is your air? Find out by checking the **lichen** (mosslike plants made of fungi and algae) that grow on bricks, trees, and stones. Thick, hairy lichen only grow in clean air. Flat lichen grow in clean air but can also survive in polluted air.

hairy lichen

flat lichen

Natural Cycles

Earth's atmosphere has remained the same for millions of years. This little-changing, or stable, atmosphere helps regulate weather around the world.

Plants and animals help maintain the balance of gases in the air. Plants add oxygen to the air as they make their own food in a process called **photosynthesis**. They **absorb** carbon dioxide (CO_2) gas, water, and minerals and make sugars using sunlight (solar energy). Plants also release oxygen as a waste product. Animals breathe in oxygen and breathe out carbon dioxide.

Plants take in carbon dioxide and give off oxygen. Animals, such as deer, breathe in oxygen and breathe out carbon dioxide gas. ▼

The Greenhouse Effect

Sunlight not only drives the weather cycles in our atmosphere but also generates warmth so life can flourish. Warmer temperatures, combined with waste gases, dust, and soot produced by people, animals, natural disasters, vehicles, and machines, help trap air pollution close to Earth. This layer of hot, dirty air creates a "greenhouse effect" that prevents the extra heat from reflecting off of Earth's surface into outer space. As a result, temperatures around Earth are on the rise as air pollution around the world increases.

TRY THIS!

Air and Sunlight

Use three jars and a thermometer to investigate the warming power of sunlight. Fill the jars with cold water and record the water temperature. Place one jar outside in the Sun, another in the shade, and the third behind a pane of glass in the Sun. After half an hour, test the water temperatures again. What do you find and why? See page 31 for the answer.

◄ **As the Sun heats Earth's surface, tiny drops of water evaporate and rise to form clouds.**

What Causes Pollution?

Any substance that harms nature by spoiling the quality of our water, soil, or air can cause pollution. Examples of pollution include sewage runoff, oil spills, factory fumes, and any buried substances that affect the soil and filter down into the groundwater.

Any material that causes pollution is called a **pollutant**. Air pollutants include chemicals in the form of gases as well as tiny particles of dust, ash, and soot. People pollute nearly every place they live, but natural disasters can also pollute. Fires started by lightning and volcanic **eruptions** are natural events that produce pollution. An erupting volcano usually shoots a giant cloud of ash and smoke into the air.

▲ Some pollution is naturally produced. When the Mount Pinatubo volcano in the Philippine Islands erupted in 1991, it covered the region with a thick, polluting layer of volcanic ash.

▲ Factories, such as this processing plant in Canada, often produce dangerous types of pollution.

Checking for Pollution

Clean, fresh air has no smell or color. We can see or smell many kinds of pollution, such as smoke billowing from a bonfire. Some of the most dangerous types of pollution, such as a natural gas (methane) leak or **nuclear radiation** (*see page* 24), are invisible and have no smell. Scientists use special instruments to check for these types of pollution.

KNOW THE FACTS

NATURAL DISASTER
For two years, the ash cloud from the 1991 eruption of Mount Pinatubo affected the world's weather. The eruption reduced the amount of sunlight and lowered average temperatures.

Industry and Energy

Earth's atmosphere has stayed nearly the same for thousands of years. For the last few centuries, however, the increasing human population has slowly changed air quality by producing more pollution. Factories and power plants are main sources of air pollution.

Factories and power plants produce pollution as they burn **fossil fuels** (coal, oil, and natural gas) for energy. The waste gases produced by fossil fuels include carbon dioxide, sulfur dioxide, and nitrogen oxides. Factories may also emit smoke, dust, soot, and airborne poisonous chemicals.

The appliances we rely on in our homes use lots of energy. Power plants cause pollution as they burn fossil fuels to produce the energy we need. ▼

A Growing Problem

People have always produced small amounts of pollution.
For example, smoky fires have provided heat for cooking,
warming homes, and powering blacksmiths' **forges** for
thousands of years. Pollution increased throughout the
nineteenth century as people invented new machinery
for manufacturing. These machines, and the fuel-powered
trains, ships, and cars that followed, produced pollution.
During the twentieth century, machine use increased,
and the human population grew more rapidly than ever.

TRY THIS! ## Soot from Fuel

Soot and grime from industry now blacken
buildings in many cities. To see how burning fuel produces
pollution, ask an adult to hold an ovenproof dish over a
lighted candle for a minute. Move the dish around slightly.
Soot will soon appear on the underside.

▲ Since the beginning
of the Industrial Age
in the late eighteenth
century, the machines
used in manufacturing
and mining processes
have burned more and
more fossil fuels.

Traffic Pollution

Cars, trucks, trains, planes, and ships all
pollute the air as they burn gasoline and
diesel fuels. Pollution levels are higher
in crowded cities than in rural areas.

Vehicles give off poisonous gases, including carbon
monoxide and nitrous oxides, as they burn fuel. Carbon
monoxide can harm your health — and even kill you —
by preventing your blood from absorbing oxygen.
Exposure to this odorless, colorless gas causes sleepiness
and headaches. Nitrous oxides help **smog** form (*see page 14*).

**Planes require a lot of fuel
to fly from place to place,
but overall, millions of cars
and trucks produce far
more air pollution. ▼**

Exhaust Fumes

Lead added to gasoline makes vehicle engines run smoothly, but lead in exhaust gases harms kidneys, brains, and nerves. Most **developed countries**, including the United States, require the use of lead-free gasoline, which causes less pollution. Cars, trucks, and buses in the United States are also fitted with devices called **catalytic converters** that clean up exhaust fumes. But road traffic increases every year, so air pollution from vehicles remains a major problem.

TRY THIS!

Family Car Use

How much gasoline does your family use in a week? Keep a record of the mileage you travel during all the car trips you make in a week. Do you do a lot of stop-and-go driving in your area? Is there a lot of other traffic? Are all your trips necessary? How can you save gasoline?

▲ People in **developing countries** have fewer vehicles, but they use leaded gasoline. Vehicle exhaust in Kuala Lumpur, Malaysia, contains dangerous lead fumes.

 KNOW THE FACTS

GAS GUZZLERS
People in developed countries own far more cars than people in poorer nations. For example, although the United States has just 5 percent of the world's population, it uses 43 percent of the world's fuel.

Smoggy Cities

Exhaust fumes from vehicles, power plants, and factories contain pollutants that can produce smog, a poisonous haze. Smog makes the air look dirty and often hides buildings and the surrounding landscape from view. Warm weather worsens this type of pollution.

Smog forms when exhaust gases react with sunlight and water vapor to produce a dangerous gas called **ozone**. The ozone layer in the upper atmosphere helps protect Earth (*see page 22*), but near the ground, ozone produces a foul-smelling, **toxic** haze. Cities located in bowl-shaped valleys trap dirty air, which makes smog a major problem.

▲ Mexico City's smog worsens in summer, when sunlight, heat, and high humidity mix with exhaust fumes. This chemical reaction can cause breathing problems and lung damage.

Health Problems

Air poisoned with smog may harm your health. It can make your eyes and throat itchy and sore and may provoke (cause) an **allergic** reaction. Certain people, such as young children and the elderly, might develop **asthma** and other lung problems from breathing polluted air. On some hot days, smog gets so bad that some people must stay indoors.

◄ **Smog hangs over Los Angeles, California.**

TAKE CARE!

Masks for Bicyclists

In many cities, smog and traffic fumes cause breathing problems for bicyclists. If you bike in a busy city, you might need a mask to filter harmful gases from the air.

Acid Rain

The burning of fossil fuels (especially coal)
releases sulfur dioxide and nitrous oxides,
gases that dissolve in moist air. This causes
a weak **sulfuric acid** rain in many regions.
Acid rain harms plants, creatures, and buildings.

Acid rain occurs when waste gases from power plants,
vehicles, and factories mix with water vapor in the air to
make a weak acid. Tiny drops of polluted water form clouds,
which later shed their moisture as acid rain, sleet, or snow.
Acid rain is especially damaging to waterways, plants, and
animals. It also harms buildings, monuments, and stone.

◄ Trees damaged by acid
rain shed their leaves or
needles and become more
likely to die from fungal
infections, diseases, or
insect infestations.

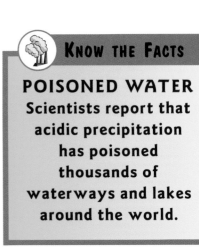

KNOW THE FACTS

POISONED WATER
Scientists report that
acidic precipitation
has poisoned
thousands of
waterways and lakes
around the world.

Drifting on the Wind

Winds can carry clouds of acid rain far from the source of pollution. For example, acid rain pollution produced in the Midwest has poisoned thousands of trees in Canada and the northeastern United States. Limestone dust sprayed on lakes and **wetlands** damaged by acid rain **neutralizes** the acid. This expensive treatment only lasts a few years.

▲ A helicopter sprays chemicals on a lake to help counteract the effects of acid rain.

TRY THIS!

Acid Damage

Acid rain damages stone, such as marble, used in tombstones. To see for yourself, soak a stick of chalk in a jar of vinegar. Chalk is a very soft form of marble. Vinegar contains a stronger concentration of acid and thus works more quickly than acid rain, but the effect of the acid on the chalk is similar to that of acid rain on marble and stone buildings.

Global Warming

Earth's average temperature is slowly but steadily getting warmer. Scientists call this condition **global warming**. They believe that air pollution contributes to this problem.

Vehicles, factories, and power plants burn fossil fuels. They release "greenhouse gases," such as carbon dioxide, that trap the Sun's heat in the atmosphere. The heat increases the atmosphere's natural "greenhouse effect" (*see pages 6–7*), raising average temperatures. Other greenhouse gases include nitrous oxides and methane. Vehicle exhaust produces nitrous oxides. Fossil fuel production and use and organic decomposition (rotting) produce methane gas.

Ice, snow, and glaciers at Earth's polar regions now melt more rapidly because of global warming. The higher melting rate leads to increased ocean levels worldwide. A glacier (below) melts into the ocean at the North Pole. ▼

Rising Waters

During the twentieth century, Earth's average temperature rose by 0.9° F (0.5° C). Temperatures may increase by another 3.6–5.4° F (2–3° C) by the year 2100. Warmer weather causes faster melting of polar ice caps and makes global sea levels rise. Global warming also brings the risk of floods to low-lying areas. If global warming increases, coastal regions such as the Florida Keys could someday end up underwater.

▲ High walls called dykes keep rising sea levels at bay in low-lying countries such as the Netherlands.

HELPING OUT | Saving Energy

Power plants that burn fossil fuels to supply us with energy release huge amounts of greenhouse gases. We can all help slow down global warming by using less energy. There are a number of different ways we can do this. For example, always turn off the lights when you leave a room. Drive less. Turn your home's thermostat down in winter and put on a sweater. In summer, turn the air conditioning to a higher temperature and dress in lighter clothing. Use your clothes dryer in consecutive cycles to conserve heat.

 KNOW THE FACTS

Developed nations use much more energy and produce more greenhouse gases than developing nations. In 2000–2001, the tons (tonnes) of carbon dioxide produced per person per year were:

United States 20.9 (19.0)
Australia   18.6 (16.9)
Canada   15.1 (13.7)
England   10.5 (9.5)
Japan   10.3 (9.3)

Changing Weather

Global warming may cause wild and more extreme weather throughout the world. Some areas may experience more flooding, while others have a greater risk of **drought**.

Studies of average temperatures and climate patterns show that global warming is changing the world's weather. Dry regions, such as parts of Africa and Australia, seem to be getting even drier, which makes disasters such as droughts and fires more likely. Elsewhere, more rain is falling on wet regions, causing more flooding. These changes make it more difficult for farmers in those areas to grow crops.

▲ Hurricanes (called "typhoons" in Southeast Asia) form over warm ocean areas and cause major damage when they sweep inland. Global warming could make these large storms more common.

◄ Colonies of small, soft-bodied animals called coral polyps secrete hard skeletons. When they die, their skeletons are left behind to build coral reefs. Colorful algae that live inside the coral polyps help create a living covering that gives the reefs a special beauty. Coral polyps thrive only at depths where sunlight can reach them and within a very narrow range of temperatures. If the water gets too hot or too cold, the coral polyps become stressed and expel their algae. (This process, called "bleaching," turns the coral white.) Bleached coral means dead coral polyps — and a sick reef.

Animal Homes

In the future, global warming may threaten the survival of animals that live in particular **habitats**, such as marshes, scrublands, or the polar regions. If conditions become unsuitable where the animals live, they may become extinct. Warmer ocean temperatures threaten sea creatures, including the delicate coral polyps that build coral reefs. Coral reefs provide protection for many different kinds of marine (saltwater) animals and plants.

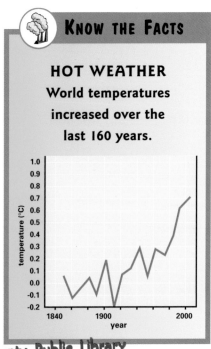

KNOW THE FACTS

HOT WEATHER
World temperatures increased over the last 160 years.

Ozone Loss

High in Earth's atmosphere, a layer of ozone gas shields us from harmful rays in sunlight. Air pollution on Earth's surface can rise and damage this protective layer.

Ozone is a colorless gas and a form of oxygen. The ozone layer is located between 12 and 30 miles (19 and 48 kilometers) above Earth's surface. Ozone acts like a natural sunscreen that shields Earth from harmful **ultraviolet (UV) rays** that can harm plants and animals and may cause skin cancer and eye damage in humans. In the 1980s, scientists discovered that an ozone "hole," or area of reduced ozone, appeared over the polar regions each year. Pollutants at ground level float up to destroy the ozone layer.

▲ The ozone "hole" over Antarctica shows up in dark blue in this 2003 satellite image.

Repairing the Damage

A group of gases called **chlorofluorocarbons** (**CFCs**) also help destroy the ozone layer. These gases were used in refrigerators, air conditioners, and many cleaning products. The CFCs also propelled contents of spray cans and helped form styrofoam cups, plates, and packaging. In 1987, some countries agreed to slowly phase out their use of CFCs. The ozone layer may recover gradually over the next fifty years.

◄ **Discarded refrigerators containing CFCs must be carefully dismantled (taken apart) to prevent the dangerous chemicals from being released into the atmosphere.**

The Global Threat

Some kinds of air pollution, such as smoke from a single cigarette, happen deliberately but occur in small amounts. Accidents cause some of the worst cases of air pollution. Whether deliberate or accidental, air pollution poses a huge global threat to people, animals, and the environment.

In 1986, an explosion at the Chernobyl nuclear plant in Ukraine spread harmful radiation over much of Europe. Some radiation also drifted over North America. ▼

Nuclear power plants, nuclear weapons, and some medical devices get their energy by splitting atoms of **radioactive** metals, such as uranium, plutonium, thorium, and cesium. Nuclear radiation can sicken or kill any living thing. In the last sixty years, nuclear weapons tests and explosions have released much invisible, deadly, radioactive pollution into the atmosphere. Accidents at nuclear power plants in Ukraine, the United States, and Japan also released clouds of nuclear radiation.

24

▲ People cut and burned this forest land in Liberia, West Africa, to make new fields for farming.

Burning Forests

Soil conditions in some parts of the developing world are so bad that farmers must constantly cut down forests in new areas for cropland. After farmers cut the trees, they dry out the branches and leaves and then start fires to clear the land. This widespread "slash-and-burn" practice harms the atmosphere by filling the air with huge clouds of smoke.

 KNOW THE FACTS

FOREST INTO FARMLAND

Thirty percent of the world's forests have been turned into farmland. Loss of forest land upsets the balance of atmospheric gases. Trees produce oxygen and absorb carbon dioxide (CO_2). Burning releases CO_2.

TAKE CARE!

Indoor Air Pollution

Smoking causes serious illnesses such as heart disease, **emphysema**, and lung cancer. Smoking cigarettes, cigars, and pipes not only harms the smoker but also affects those nearby who breathe in the secondhand smoke. Don't smoke. Avoid breathing in other people's smoke!

Tackling Air Pollution

We can tackle air pollution by cleaning up any damage that has already occurred. But the best solution for cleaner air is to pollute less in the first place. All over the world, governments, scientists, and ordinary people are working to prevent air pollution.

Global warming is a very serious, worldwide problem. Special international conferences, called Earth Summits, meet frequently to find ways of solving the crisis. At the Kyoto Summit in Japan in 1997, representatives drew up a plan to reduce greenhouse gases by 5 percent by 2012. Two of the world's biggest polluters, the United States and Russia, refused to sign the Kyoto Protocol because they fear it would cost their industries too much money.

Wind farms provide energy without polluting. Unlike fossil fuel sources, wind energy will never run out. Problems with wind farms include finding large tracts of open land with steady winds, keeping birds safe from the blades, and providing a pleasant landscape. ▼

28

◄ This **solar-powered** car in California is having its battery recharged by sunlight. Solar cars do not use gasoline and do not produce harmful exhaust gases.

"Clean" Energy

Global warming is mainly caused by burning **nonrenewable** fossil fuels — once used, they are gone forever. We can slow down global warming by using "clean" energy that pollutes very little or not at all. Sunlight, wind, and flowing water are **renewable** resources that provide a constant supply of energy without adding to the global warming problem.

27

Get Involved!

Everyone can help reduce air pollution by using energy more carefully and burning fewer fossil fuels. Walking, riding a bike, or traveling by bus or train instead of private car cuts air pollution and saves precious fuel.

Every day, you can do your small part to help prevent air pollution created by fossil fuel use. Reading or studying near a window cuts down on your need for electric lights. Ask your parents to keep their cars properly tuned and to install insulation in your home to cut fuel use (and fuel bills). Simple actions, such as not leaving the refrigerator door open and taking a shower instead of a bath, also save energy.

▲ **If we travel everywhere by car, we use a lot of gasoline, which pollutes the air. School buses and other forms of public transportation help cut fossil fuel use.**

Recycling

Fossil fuels are used in the production of the packaging that protects food and other merchandise. Do you ever think about all the packaging that you throw away? Recycling paper, plastic, glass, cans, cardboard, and even old clothing, such as coats, sweaters, and jeans, saves natural resources. Buy recycled products if possible, such as paper towels and toilet tissue. That may not seem like much, but if we all make small changes, it will make a big difference.

◄ **Recycling paper, plastic, glass, and cans is a good way to save energy, cut air pollution, and help slow global warming. Ask your school to start a recycling program. Buy products for school and home that use less disposable packaging.**

HELPING OUT

Share a Ride

Reduce air pollution by using less gasoline to get to school. If you live far from school and there is no school bus, ask your parents to set up a car pool schedule with others in your neighborhood.

Glossary

absorb to take in.

allergic related to a bodily response to substances such as pollen or mold.

asthma an illness that affects the lungs and airways and makes breathing difficult.

catalytic converters devices fitted to vehicle exhaust systems that reduce the amount of air pollution produced.

chlorofluorocarbons (CFCs) gases used in the manufacture of refrigerators, air conditioners, aerosol (spray) cans, and foam packaging that harm the ozone layer.

developed countries richer countries with well-developed industries.

developing countries poorer countries with less well-developed industries.

drought a long period of time without rain.

emphysema a serious, fatal lung disease usually caused by smoking.

eruptions explosions that spew lava, ash, gas, and other natural debris from a volcano.

forges workshops where metal is heated and pounded or poured into different shapes.

fossil fuels fuels, such as coal, oil, and natural gas, that formed from the fossilized remains of plants and animals.

global warming the worldwide rise in average annual temperatures caused by pollution and some natural disasters.

habitats particular types of environments in which plants and animals live.

lichen an organism that resembles moss but is a combination of a fungus and an alga.

neutralize to counteract or make harmless.

nonrenewable cannot be replaced.

nuclear having to do with atoms and their nuclei (central parts) or with atomic energy.

nuclear radiation the harmful, invisible rays and particles produced by the breakup of atomic nuclei.

ozone a form of oxygen. The ozone layer in the upper atmosphere absorbs harmful (UV) rays in sunlight. Ozone that forms from air pollution near the ground is harmful to all living creatures.

photosynthesis the process by which plants make food using sunlight, water, and carbon dioxide gas from the air.

polar regions the areas surrounding Earth's northernmost and southernmost reaches.

pollutant a substance that changes and harms the air, water, or land.

pollution the results of harmful substances that damage the environment.

power plants factories that produce energy, usually by burning fossil fuels, such as coal, natural gas, or oil, to create electricity.

radioactive the state of giving off radiation and energy through the breakup of atoms.

renewable replaceable.

smog a poisonous haze caused by vehicle, power plant, and industrial exhaust fumes mixing with hot, humid, stationary air masses, usually in a bowl-shaped valley.

solar-powered powered by sunlight.

sulfuric acid an acid produced by the burning of coal during energy production.

toxic poisonous.

ultraviolet (UV) rays the part of solar radiation that tans and burns our skin.

wetlands areas of very wet soil, sometimes with freshwater ponds or swamps.

Further Information

Books

Acid Rain. Earth Watch (series). Sally Morgan (Heinemann)

Acid Rain. Our Planet in Peril (series). Louise Petheram
    (Bridgestone Books)

Air Pollution: Our Impact on the Planet. 21st Century Debate (series).
    Matthew Chapman and Rob Bowden (Raintree)

Changing Climate. Precious Earth (series). Jen Green (Chrysalis Education)

Conservation and Natural Resources. Our Planet Earth (series).
    Discovery Channel School Science (Gareth Stevens)

Global Pollution. Face the Facts (series). Paul Brown (Heinemann)

Global Warming. Science at the Edge (series). Sally Morgan (Heinemann)

Global Warming: The Threat of Earth's Changing Climate. Laurence Pringle
    (SeaStar Books)

Polluted Planet. Precious Earth (series). Jen Green (Chrysalis Education)

Weather and Climate. Our Planet Earth (series).
    Discovery Channel School Science (Gareth Stevens)

Air Pollution Web Sites

Air Pollution Quiz
www.pca.state.mn.us/kids/kidsQuizAir.cfm

Environmental Kids Club
www.epa.gov/kids/air.htm

The EPA Global Warming Kids Page
www.epa.gov/globalwarming/kids/

What is Air Pollution?
www.lbl.gov/Education/ELSI/pollution-defined.html

What is Ozone?
www.dnr.state.wi.us/org/caer/ce/eek/earth/air/ozonlayr.htm

Answer to question on page 7:
The temperature of the water in the jar left in the Sun will be warmer
than the temperature of the water in the jar left in the shade. The jar
behind the pane of glass will be warmest of all because the glass helps
trap even more of the Sun's heat rays, just as in a greenhouse.

Index

Numbers in **bold** refer to illustrations.